Mother Teresa

Mother Teresa

Caroline Lazo

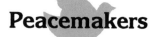

Peacemakers

DILLON PRESS
New York

Maxwell Macmillan Canada
Toronto

Maxwell Macmillan International
New York Oxford Singapore Sydney

To Anzle

Photo Credits

All photos courtesy of AP—Wide World Photos

Book design by Carol Matsuyama

Library of Congress Cataloging-in-Publication Data

Lazo, Caroline Evensen.
    Mother Teresa / Caroline Lazo. — 1st ed.
        p.   cm. — (Peacemakers)
    Includes bibliographical references and index.
    Summary: A biography of the nun who founded the Missionaries of Charity, gained wide recognition for her work with the destitute and dying in Calcutta and elsewhere, and was awarded the Nobel Peace Prize in 1979.
    ISBN 0-87518-559-2
    1. Teresa, Mother, 1910-   —Juvenile literature. 2. Missionaries of Charity—Biography—Juvenile literature. 3. Nuns—India—Calcutta—Biography—Juvenile literature. [1.Teresa, Mother, 1910-   2. Missionaries of Charity. 3. Nuns. 4. Missionaries.] I. Title. II. Series.
BX4406.5.Z8L39   1993
271'.97—dc20   92-23765
[B]

Dillon Press   Maxwell Macmillan Canada, Inc.
Macmillan Publishing Company   1200 Eglinton Avenue East
866 Third Avenue   Suite 200
New York, NY 10022   Don Mills, Ontario M3C 3N1

Macmillan Publishing Company is part of the Maxwell Communication Group of Companies.

First Edition

Printed in the United States of America

10   9   8   7   6   5   4   3   2   1

Contents

Introduction..6

Freedom . . . and Problems................................9

Family Ties..13

A Symbol of Joy..15

The First Call..18

Like the Moon..23

A New Life, a New Name..25

The Crowning Point..28

Over the Garden Wall..33

Into the Heart of Calcutta..36

Duty Was Joy..41

The Word Spreads..46

A Prayer for Peace..54

A Messenger of Love..59

For Further Reading..62

Index..63

Introduction

In 1948, the year Mahatma Gandhi died, another great teacher began a mission of peace and hope in India. She became known throughout the world as Mother Teresa, but in the streets of Calcutta she was (and still is) called a living saint.

Like Gandhi, Mother Teresa left a life of comfort to live and work among the poor and to show by example the power of love. "Love one another," she said, "because it is the only way to peace." Like Gandhi, she turned her words into actions, and in 1950 she founded a new Catholic order, the Missionaries of Charity. Her mission, she said, was to care for "the poorest of the poor," and she had no trouble finding them in Calcutta—an area of poverty unlike any other in India, or probably the world.

With only 12 sisters (Catholic nuns) she began to help—and to house—thousands of sick children who had been sleeping and dying in alleys throughout the city. She found lepers there, too, who had been abandoned and left to die in the streets. People with leprosy had been treated as outcasts and called "untouchables," but Mother Teresa comforted them and, like Gandhi, treated them with the same respect as she did with everyone else. "They are

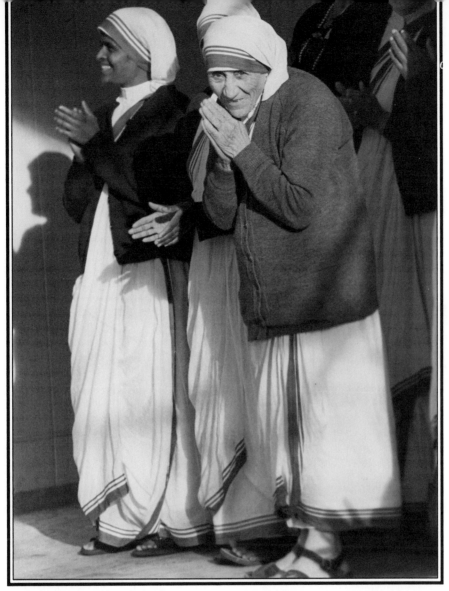

Mother Teresa has been spreading her message of love and peace for almost 50 years.

children of God," she said, "and when you love them, you love God Himself."

Though she is quiet, gentle, and fragile-looking, Mother

Teresa delivers a strong message wherever she goes—to citizens and heads of state alike: "Look around you," she says. "Even the richest countries in the world are plagued with poverty. Poverty begins when sharing stops. . . . And now there are lonely and homeless people everywhere."

In spite of a bad heart condition, she continues to care for the sick, the lonely, and the dying all over the world. She has been awarded some of the world's highest honors, including the Nobel Peace Prize, though she claims that thousands of others are more worthy of such praise.

Is she a living saint? She would say no, because she refuses to take credit for her remarkable achievements. "They are gifts from God," she says. And she credits her loving parents for showing by their own example the joy that comes from helping others and the peace that comes from prayer.

Wherever she travels—from the streets of Calcutta to the halls of Harvard University to the United Nations General Assembly—Mother Teresa urges people to pray.

"Prayer cleanses the heart," she says, "and leads to peace."

Freedom . . . and Problems

When India was ruled by Great Britain, foreign mission-aries were common in India. *Too* common, according to many Hindus there. Some Hindus, including Mahatma Gandhi, resented outsiders who tried to convert their country to Christianity—regardless of the traditions and deep feelings of the people. But Mother Teresa would give new meaning to missionary work and change India's image of it forever.

Indians longed for independence from the British Empire because the British had oppressed them for so many years and had made them slaves in their own country. When they finally won their freedom in 1947, the Indians were glad to see the British officers and emissaries leave their land.

But with independence came internal problems. Pakistan, formerly part of India, became a separate Muslim country, and in order to stay in India and escape Muslim control, thousands fled south. Many went to Calcutta—the most important seaport on India's east coast—where more than nine million people live today. Hundreds more settled there to escape famine and floods in other areas. But they found no comfort in the

An Indian boy fingers Mother Teresa's rosary as she makes a tour of his village.

most overcrowded city in the world.

Many thousands slept on rags in the streets, and because of a lack of sewers and safe water supplies, hundreds became ill every day . . . and died unnoticed. Few outsiders dared to enter the heart of Calcutta, where filth and disease—especially leprosy—were so rampant.

"It's a hellhole here," a reporter wrote. "I don't know anyone—except maybe Superman—who could help these hopeless people."

He didn't know Mother Teresa!

Family Ties

Mother Teresa was born on August 26, 1910, in Skopje, Macedonia, now a part of Yugoslavia. Her parents, originally from Albania, named her Agnes Gonxha (*Agnes* meaning lamb, and *Gonxha* meaning flower bud). But later, when she became a nun, Agnes followed an old Catholic tradition and adopted the name of a saint she admired. She named herself Teresa after St. Thérèse, a 19th-century French nun honored by Catholics for her remarkable courage during a long and painful terminal illness.

Agnes's parents, Drana and Nikola Bojaxhiu (pronounced *Boy-ya-jee-oo*), were both strict and compassionate with their three children—Aga, Lazar, and Agnes. Aga would one day become a journalist, and Lazar would find a career in the army. "We were a family full of joy," Agnes recalled later, "and we children were happy and contented."

Much of their joy came from church activities shared by all the family and close friends. Their Catholic faith would continue to tie them together, even when living apart. Like the sun, it was always there, visible or not. Agnes and her sister sang in the church choir in Skopje

Mother Teresa's smile expresses the joy she spreads to those around her.

and were known as "the two nightingales." Agnes often sang solos and could play the accordion and mandolin as well. No wonder her friends thought she was destined for stardom in the field of music! But her mother's compassion and constant desire to help others—even strangers who came to the house—would have the greatest impact on Agnes's future.

Drana and Nikola Bojaxhiu's house was open to friends and relatives day and night. Together they kept their Albanian heritage—language and customs—alive in Skopje. Agnes never forgot the lively gatherings where her parents sang patriotic songs, laughed, and shared memories of Albania. Her parents also welcomed missionaries and priests to their house, and even as a little girl, Agnes loved to listen to these visitors' reports of life in far-off places and showed concern about the suffering they had seen—especially in India.

Nikola was a co-owner of a construction company, and a generous man. He often ordered Lazar to bring money, food, and clothing to the poor in Skopje, and he helped to provide shelter for them as well. Both Drana and Nikola were well known and loved in the community because of their many acts of kindness. And Agnes would always remember her mother's words: "When you do good, do it without display, as if you were tossing a pebble into the sea." And her father's advice became part of Agnes's own philosophy later on: "Never take a morsel of food that you are not ready to share with others."

Nikola was strict with his three children, insisting on high standards in their schoolwork and stressing compassion toward others less fortunate than they were. Agnes adored her father, and his sudden death when she was only eight was a major turning point in her childhood and family life.

A Symbol of Joy

Hundreds attended Nikola's funeral—including fellow Catholics, city officials, and many others representing a variety of religions and cultures. Turks, Greeks, and Albanians came to say farewell to a man they loved. The mixture of people in Nikola's life was an important factor

When she was younger, Mother Teresa learned to respect other people and cultures.

in Agnes's life, too. She learned that people of all backgrounds can live together in peace if they love and respect one another. And if they can have harmony at home, she thought, why can't they have it around the world? She believed they could . . . and would happily spend her life showing them how.

Following Nikola's funeral, Drana gathered her three children together and reminded them that with God's help they would carry on—and continue to find joy in helping others, as their father had done. When her income from his company ran out, she turned her sewing skills into a moneymaking business. Though her income from dressmaking was small, it was enough to support her family. Big parties came to a halt, but the Bojaxhiu house remained open to friends and relatives—and all those in need. Later, Mother Teresa recalled those times:

> Many of the poor in Skopje knew our house, and none left it empty-handed. We had guests at table every day. At first I used to ask, "Who are they?" and Mother would answer: "Some are relatives, but all of them are our people." When I was older, I realized that the strangers were poor people who had nothing and whom my mother was feeding.

The church became a stronger family tie than ever before. Agnes, her brother, and her sister prayed with their mother every evening; and they loved to participate in the festivals and retreats, especially the annual trip to Letnice, where Catholics worshiped the Madonna of Letnice. Located in the mountains of Montenegro, the area had just the right climate for Agnes, who was a delicate child and prone to illness.

Agnes always looked forward to the ride—in a horse-drawn carriage—to Letnice. She and her sister, Aga, knew there was fun in store for them as well as time for worship and prayer. There would be games, storytelling, and long walks in the mountains—enjoyed by Christians from many different churches, not just Catholic ones. For Agnes, Letnice would always be a symbol of the joy that comes from loving and caring about others, and a reminder of the fun she had in her childhood! But above all, Letnice was a place where family and church—the two strongest influences in her life—came together.

The First Call

Agnes was only 12 years old when she first thought of becoming a nun and devoting her life to the church.

Later she reminisced about those formative years:

> For six years I thought and prayed about it. . . . But in the end I had the assurance that God really was calling me. Our Lady of Letnice helped me to understand this.

Local priests, particularly Father Jambrekovich, also helped direct her decision.

Soon after Father Jambrekovich arrived in Skopje, he formed the Sodality of the Sisters of Mary—a church group that kept in touch with missionaries around the world. Agnes joined the group and began to hear firsthand reports of the terrible conditions in the slums, or *bustees*, of India. She read more about them in *Catholic Missions*, a magazine Father Jambrekovich had brought to her church. Though she had dreamed of being a teacher or pursuing a career in music, Agnes began to realize that serving others was more important. And at the age of 18 she announced her decision to become a missionary nun.

Her decision shocked her brother, Lazar, who had become an officer in the army of Albania's King Zog. He wrote to her immediately: "Are you crazy? How can you leave your happy home life to live in some poor country so far away from all you have known?"

Agnes wrote back: "You think you are so important—serving the king of two million subjects. Well, I am serving the King of the whole world! Which of us do you think is in the better place?"

After he thought about it, Lazar realized that her decision was the right one. He could remember how Agnes had always enjoyed helping the slow students in school, when she was at the top of her class; how she loved to help her mother with the poor who came to their house in Skopje; and how she admired her mother's endless patience, compassion, and devotion to God. She even looked like her mother! She had large, clear eyes that seemed translucent, and while she was physically frail (except for her hands, which were unusually strong), she always seemed happy. And friends said her smile was contagious.

Agnes's decision to enter a convent did not surprise her mother; she was well aware of her daughter's devotion to the church and her compassion for others. Still, with her son far away in the army, Drana was not happy about

Mother Teresa entered a convent much like this one when she was 18 years old.

saying good-bye to Agnes, too. She knew Agnes's goal was missionary work in India, which meant she might never see her again. But once she sensed Agnes's total commitment, she accepted the decision with her usual grace. "My daughter," she told Agnes, "if you begin something, begin it wholeheartedly . . . and strive only for God."

Agnes also received strong support from Aga and her friends at school, as well as from the priests. "Joy that comes from the depths of your being is like a compass, by which you can tell what direction your life should follow," one priest told her.

In 1928 Agnes made her last trip to Letnice, where she prayed at the shrine of the Madonna. And after many farewell parties in Skopje, she prepared to leave for her religious training at the Loreto Abbey in Dublin, Ireland, where her new life as a Catholic sister would begin. She chose the Order of Loreto because its missionaries were working in Bengal, in eastern India—her ultimate destination. But she would soon discover there was much to learn before she could sail for India . . . that "poor country," as Lazar had written, "so far away from all you have known."

Like the Moon

On September 25, 1928, Agnes began the long trip to Dublin. Many friends came to the train station to say good-bye, and *Catholic Missions,* her favorite magazine, covered the story:

> She was the life and soul of the Catholic girls' activities and the church choir, and it was generally acknowledged that her departure would leave an enormous gap. When she left Skopje, about a hundred people were at the station to see her off. They were all in tears and greatly moved.

And Lorenzo Antoni, a friend and music teacher, recorded the event in his diary:

> The train began to move. On the platform we stood waving our handkerchiefs, and she waved back as long as we could see her. The distant sunlight illuminated her briefly, and she seemed to us like the moon slowly vanishing in the light of day; growing smaller and smaller, still waving, still vanishing. And then we saw her no more.

On board the train, Agnes met Betika Kajnc, who was

Mother Teresa's desire to devote herself to helping the poor came after much thought and prayer.

also traveling to the Loreto Abbey. Like Agnes, Betika had given up her home life—and any thought of marriage and having children of her own—to follow God's will and to work only for Him.

By the time the young women arrived in Dublin, they had become good friends . . . and were ready for the biggest adventure of their lives.

A New Life, a New Name

Though Agnes's training at Loreto Abbey lasted only six weeks, it was the first major step toward achieving her goal to become a missionary nun in India. It was a time full of firsts. For the first time she wore the "habit"—the dress of the Loreto nuns. She took her first course in the English language. And it was the first time she would use the name Teresa.

Learning English was essential, because from 1858 to 1947 India was governed by Britain. Teresa had always been a good student, so learning a new language was not difficult. Later, in India, she would master Hindi and Bengali—native Indian languages—as well.

While preparing to be Loreto nuns, the young women learned the importance of silence and how to listen intently as sisters read aloud from the Bible. Their "Great Silence," as it was called, lasted from bedtime until morning, when they joined together for Mass and Communion. Teresa studied hard and welcomed her new life with enthusiasm, but teachers noticed nothing unusual about her—no special signs of the greatness she would achieve. She was "shy and hardworking," one sister recalled, and everyone liked her.

Mother Teresa dedicates a new convent for her Missionaries of Charity.

On December 1, 1928, Teresa and her friend Betika, now called Mary Magdalene, set sail for India to continue their training at the Loreto convent in Darjeeling. The trip was long and the sea was rough, but their spirits were high as they approached their destination. Teresa, now an ardent letter writer, kept *Catholic Missions* up-to-date on her travels:

> When our ship docked, we sang a silent *Te Deum*. On the quayside our Indian Sisters were waiting for us, and with a joy which I cannot describe, we touched the soil of Bengal for the first time. . . . Here we shall stay for a week; then we shall go on to Darjeeling, where we shall remain for the whole of our novitiate. Pray for us a great deal, that we may become good and courageous missionaries.

On May 23, 1929, Teresa became a novice (a new member of the Loreto order) and her new name became official. After two years of intensive study of Loreto history, prayer, and mission work, she took her first vows—promising to live a life of poverty, chastity, and obedience—and was ready to teach at the convent school in Darjeeling.

The Crowning Point

For centuries Darjeeling, located on the slopes of the Himalayan Mountains, has been known for its tea and healthy climate. When the British ruled India, the governor of Bengal and other British officials spent their summers there, and it became a famous resort for the rich.

Darjeeling was also known as an educational center, and though she had little time for tea and mountain air, Sister Teresa enjoyed teaching at the convent there. In fact, she also assisted the nurses in a Bengali hospital, where for the first time she came face-to-face with the relentless human suffering she had heard and read about. *Catholic Missions* published her report of a typical day there:

> The tiny veranda is always full of the sick, the wretched, and the miserable. All eyes are fixed, full of hope, on me. Mothers give me their sick children. . . . Then comes a young man who has been stabbed in the back by some delinquent in a quarrel. Finally, a man arrives with a bundle from which two dry twigs protrude. They are the legs of a child. The little boy is very weak. I realize he is near death and hurry to bring holy

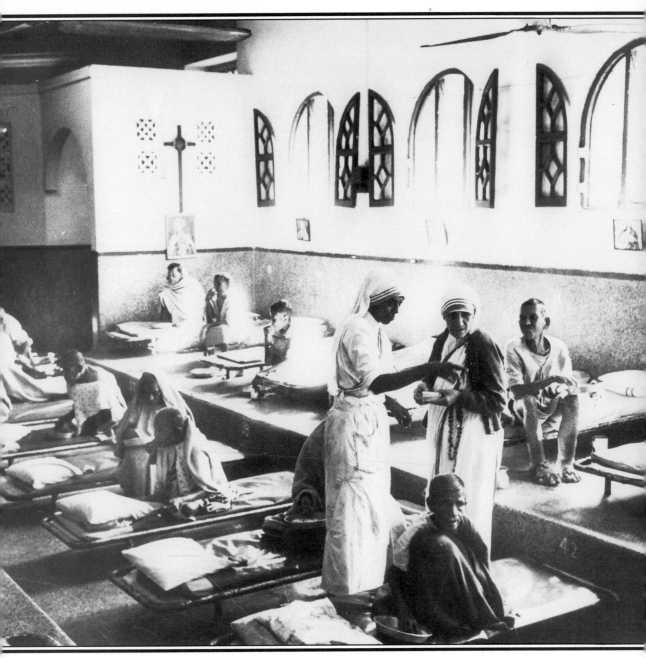

Mother Teresa's love for the poor of India came about while working in hospitals like this one.

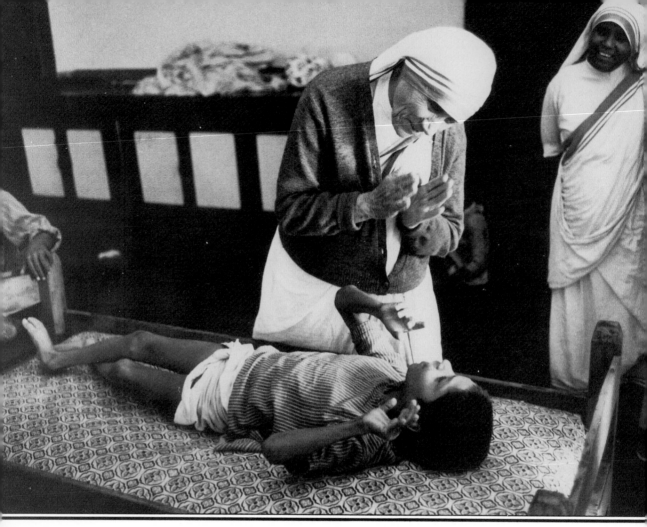

Mother Teresa visits a child in an Indian hospital.

water. The man is afraid that we do not want to take the child, and says, "If you do not want him, I will throw him into the grass. The jackals will not turn up their noses at him." My heart freezes. The poor child! Weak, and blind—totally blind. With much pity and love I take the little one into my arms, and fold him in my apron. The child has found a second mother. "Who so receives a child, receives me," said the Divine Friend of all little ones. The incident of the blind child is the crowning point of my working day.

But even those days in the hospital could not compare to the horrifying, massive misery she would find in Calcutta years later. Would she be prepared for such difficult work? No one who worked with her had any doubts. Writer David Porter summed up Sister Teresa's special qualities that seemed to predict her remarkable future success: "All those who observed Teresa seem to have been impressed by . . . a deeply spiritual attitude to suffering and poverty, and an energy and practical authority which enabled her to make her vision a reality."

Her next assignment—to teach geography and history at St. Mary's School in Calcutta—would bring her closer to that reality and to her goal.

Over the Garden Wall

St. Mary's School was located in Entally, a poor section of Calcutta, but its beautiful gardens and high stone walls served as a barricade to the poverty outside. Sister Teresa loved teaching there, and she became immensely popular with the students and other sisters as well. But her work was not confined to St. Mary's. She organized classes at nearby St. Teresa's—in the slum area of the city—too. It was the daily walk outside the garden walls to St. Teresa's that prepared her and strengthened her for the enormous task ahead.

The first day at St. Teresa's was the hardest, because she didn't know what to expect. She did know that a white woman in that area was a rarity . . . as she later noted in her journal:

> When they saw me for the first time, the children wondered whether I was an evil spirit or a goddess! . . . I rolled up my sleeves immediately, rearranged the whole room, found water and a broom and began to sweep the floor. This greatly astonished them. They had never seen a schoolmistress start lessons like that, particularly because in India cleaning is something that the

The young people of India have deep respect and love for Mother Teresa.

lower castes do; and they stood staring at me for a long time. Seeing me cheerful and smiling, the girls began to help me, and the boys brought me more water. After two hours that room was . . . transformed into a clean schoolroom. It was a long room . . . originally a chapel and is now divided into five classes. . . . When I arrived there were 52 children, and now there are over 300. . . . When I first saw where the children slept and ate, I was full of anguish. It is not possible to find worse poverty.

In May 1937, Sister Teresa took her final vows, and at the same time was appointed head of St. Mary's School. From then on, she would be known as Mother Teresa. She accepted her new responsibilities with joy and grace—as her mother, Drana, had taught her so many years before. Teresa continued to share her new life with her family through letter writing and prayer. Both Aga and Lazar had returned to Albania to live, and Drana later joined them there. "I am sorry not to be with you," Teresa wrote her mother, "but be happy, dearest Mother, because your Agnes is happy." Drana wrote back and asked Teresa to

A group of Indian women gather to speak with Mother Teresa.

recall the reason she chose to be a missionary nun—to help the poorest of the poor, including the lonely and forgotten.

At the same time, Teresa was becoming more aware that a great section of Calcutta was being ignored. Hundreds were dying there every day—alone, forgotten. She knew she had to do more; she *wanted* to do more. But could she leave the comfort of the school environment, where everyone loved her? And if her brother Lazar thought she was crazy for entering a convent, what would he think of her wanting to enter—and work in—the most dangerous streets in the world? And live there!

Her questions would soon be answered, and the work for which she has become world-famous would begin.

Into the Heart of Calcutta

On September 10, 1946, Mother Teresa traveled by train to her annual retreat, and the trip changed the rest of her life. While on the train, she heard the voice of God. It was a "call within a call," she said, because the first call—to devote her life to the church—had come years before. This time it was a specific command, as she told her spiritual director:

> I was certain that He was calling me. The message was clear: I must leave the convent to help the poor by living among them. This was a command, something to be done, something definite. I knew where I had to be.

From that moment on, Mother Teresa sought support from her superiors—including the Pope himself—who finally approved her leaving the Loreto order to move into the heart of Calcutta. But before she could start an entirely new order of nuns to fulfill her mission, she would have to draft a constitution and present it to the Vatican in Rome for approval. With the help of priests and other experts, she wrote the draft and sent it to Rome.

While waiting for official approval, she decided to get more medical experience and training at the Medical Missionaries' Hospital in Patna, 200 miles away. She knew such training would be invaluable in dealing with the variety of problems in Calcutta, and by December 1948 she had completed her course and was ready to put her training and her principles into action. Wearing the white cotton sari with blue border—the dress of the poor women in India—Mother Teresa returned to Calcutta and to her new home . . . the slums of the city.

Thousands of refugees had come into the city from other parts of India. Forced out by famine and floods and political turmoil, they hoped to find better conditions in Calcutta, India's largest seaport. Many were too ill to travel beyond the city's outskirts—the Motijhil slums— where conditions were the worst of all.

When Mother Teresa walked into the Motijhil area, she was not surprised to be stared at with suspicion. She remembered the little children in Entally who helped her clean the chapel and turn it into a school. And she would win the hearts of the people in Motijhil just as she had done there. But this time she needed other nuns to help her. She prayed for them to come, though she knew the enormous sacrifice they would have to make. To leave the comfort of St. Mary's School and the beauty of the convent gardens to live among the sick and dying in the streets of

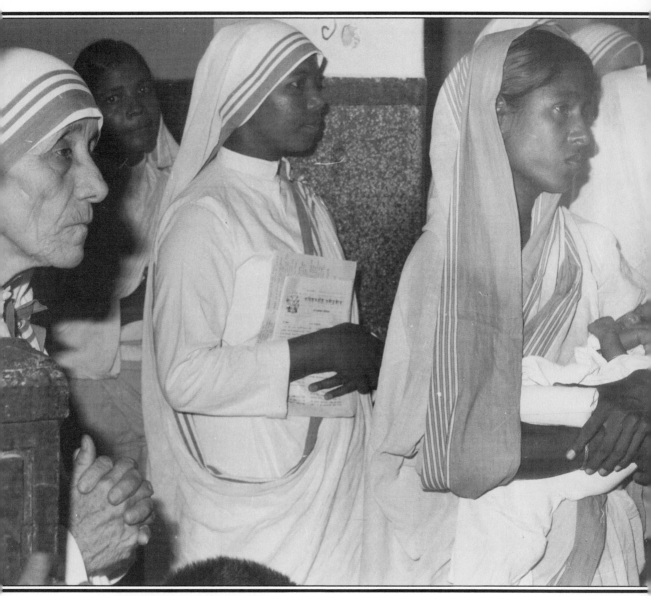

Mother Teresa with some of the young women who make up her Missionaries of Charity order

Calcutta would take unusual dedication.

But it was one of her students at St. Mary's who first answered Teresa's call. Subhasini Das, who came from a wealthy family, told Mother Teresa that she wanted to spend her life helping the poorest of the poor. She replaced her beautiful sari with the familiar white one with the blue border, and she changed her name to Agnes—after Mother Teresa, the saint she admired!

By 1950, 12 nuns had joined Mother Teresa, and in the fall of that year Pope Pius XII approved the foundation of the Order of the Missionaries of Charity. Its constitution, drafted by Mother Teresa, clearly stated the order's mission:

> Our special mission is to work for the salvation ... of the poorest of the poor. . . . God is love. The missionary must be a missionary of *love*, must always be full of love in his soul and must also spread it to the souls of others, whether Christian or not.

As more nuns joined the new order, larger space was needed to house them. Rooms donated by friends would no longer do. Finally the Catholic church bought the residence of a Muslim leader who moved to Pakistan; it was just where Mother Teresa wanted to be—right in the middle of the city. Once again, her prayers seemed to have been answered, and the former Muslim residence was transformed into the Mother House, or headquarters, for the Missionaries of Charity. The address, 54A Lower Circular Road, soon became famous in India and, eventually, around the world.

Duty Was Joy

Like the poor they served, the Missionaries of Charity ate little and owned next to nothing. Dr. William Jay Jacobs described their daily routine at the Mother House in Calcutta:

> They rose at 4:40 A.M. and immediately went to chapel for prayer. For breakfast they ate the simple Indian flat bread, *chapati*. From 8 A.M. to

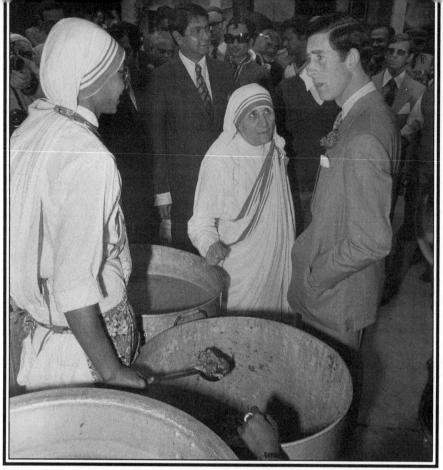

Mother Teresa shows Britain's Prince Charles one of the food distribution centers her order runs in Calcutta.

12:30 they served the poor. Following lunch came meditation and prayer and then service to the poor again until 7:30 P.M. Supper was followed by evening prayers at 9:00 and bed at 9:45.

Wherever Mother Teresa walked, people followed her. She witnessed robberies and stabbings and saw little children playing in human excrement. She saw old people huddled in doorways crying in pain. And she saw abandoned children everywhere. She turned the first open space she saw into an outdoor school. Five children joined her the first day, and more came every day thereafter. Soon she was teaching 40 children the Bengali alphabet and showing them how to use a bar of soap, which they had never seen before. Cleanliness can fight off disease, she taught them.

In 1954 Mother Teresa faced her biggest challenge—to find a home for the dying. Why should people have to die in the streets? Making them comfortable on piles of straw or rags was not good enough. She said that "people who have lived like animals" must be able "to die like angels—loved and wanted." They must die with dignity. At last, city officials agreed and gave her rooms in the back of a Hindu temple where she could comfort the dying and give them their last rites.

At first, local Hindus were angry about Mother Teresa's use of a Hindu temple (though it had been vacant a long time); they feared she would try to teach Christianity there, and that would be wrong. But when they saw her gently sprinkle water from the Ganges River on a dying

Mother Teresa helps a dying man to reach Nirmal Hriday.

man's lips, they quickly changed their minds. They respected her for knowing—and performing—that ancient Hindu rite. And they never questioned her use of the temple again. The new home for the dying was named *Nirmal Hriday* (Place of the Pure Heart), and people of all faiths and cultures were cared for there. The sisters read from the Koran to dying Muslims, because Missionaries of Charity believed every person deserved to die "loved and wanted"—and, as their constitution stated, "whether Christian or not."

As head of the new order, Mother Teresa's official title was "Reverend Mother." But that name, she said, created too much distance between her and the younger sisters, so she insisted on being called, simply, Mother. The sisters adored her; they knew she would never ask them to do a chore—no matter how rough or dirty—that she would not do herself. After carrying the dying through the streets and settling them in the Nirmal Hriday, they would spend hours sponging them off, cleaning off the bugs and dirt from the gutters the dying people were found in. Like all the sisters, Mother Teresa scrubbed the floors and hand-washed clothes and bedding every day, too. And she did everything with joy in her heart, as she was taught in childhood. Indian poet Rabindranath Tagore seemed to have Mother Teresa in mind when he wrote his famous lines:

> I slept and dreamt
> That life was joy
> I awoke and saw
> That life was duty
> I acted and behold
> Duty was joy.

The Word Spreads

Volunteers from all over India began to come to Calcutta to help Mother Teresa. They brought supplies, bedding, clothes, and food, and doctors gave them medicine as well as expert advice. A volunteer named Ann Blaikie was especially helpful: She brought all her friends together and started a clothes drive for Mother Teresa's "poorest of the poor." Ann's group became known as the Co-workers, and today there are Co-workers all over the world.

As more nuns joined the order and more volunteers gave their time, Mother Teresa could concentrate on perhaps the saddest problem of all in Calcutta: the sick and abandoned babies. She found them in trash piles, sometimes wrapped in rags to hide them. So in 1955, with the help of her sisters and others, Mother Teresa established *Shishu Bhavan* (Home for Children), a home for these babies and children. Many who were expected to die improved almost immediately after they were brought to the children's home. "It should have been named 'The Miracle House,'" a visiting doctor said. And when they were completely well, the babies were often adopted by families in Europe—thanks to Mother Teresa's efforts to find happy homes for them. She personally arranged each adoption. She even planned weddings for those who grew up in Shishu Bhavan! But that wasn't surprising, because "they are my family," she said.

Those who couldn't be saved died in the arms of the loving sisters and their Mother who saw in each child's face the image of God. No child died more loved or more wanted than those in Shishu Bhavan.

"When I saw Mother Teresa with a wounded child stretched across her lap," an observer once wrote, "I saw Michelangelo's famous sculpture of the Virgin Mary with Christ on her lap [*Pietà*] come to life . . . right before my eyes!"

A few years later, in 1957, the Missionaries of Charity opened *Shanti Nagar* (Place of Peace), a home for those suffering from leprosy. For centuries lepers had been ostracized from society because people were certain that just by touching a leper they would get the disease. Mother Teresa was not afraid. Nor were her sisters. They soothed the patients who had lost fingers and toes and other parts of their bodies to the dreaded disease. In the early stages of the illness, the sisters taught patients how

Some of the many faces of Shishu Bhavan

to accept their fate, improve their lives, and even work in spite of it! And they taught everything with a smile. "Smiling," Teresa said, "is the beginning of love."

News of Mother Teresa's amazing success spread beyond India to the rest of the world. Nuns from other cities joined her order and under her direction opened houses in Europe and the United States. She established treatment centers for drug addicts and alcoholics, too. And in 1962, in response to the large number of men who wanted to join her mission, she organized the Missionary Brothers of Charity.

Any money donated to Mother Teresa's cause was instantly put into the maintenance of her houses. Even when offered money to install carpeting in her own living quarters, Mother Teresa asked that it be spent on medicine for the sick instead. "The life of a nun, especially a life like this," she once told a young girl, "demands a spirit of sacrifice. You must forget yourself so that you can dedicate yourself to God and your neighbor."

In 1964 Pope Paul VI visited India and was given a white Lincoln Continental limousine for his tour. Before he left the country, he presented the car as a gift to Mother Teresa, to help her get around in the city. But Mother Teresa promptly raffled it off for more than $100,000 and used the profits to benefit the lepers in Shanti Nagar!

Asking for financial help was forbidden by Mother Teresa. She believed that each person can help by giving of himself or herself through work and by sharing with others. Poverty happens, she said, when people stop sharing. "And it is not how much we give that matters," she said. "It is the amount of love behind the giving that counts."

Throughout the 1960s, new houses opened in places as far away as Venezuela, Tanzania, and Australia. But shocking as it may seem, not every country welcomed Mother Teresa. Albania, her parents' homeland, was one. After World War II (1939–1945), Albania became an atheistic country—a satellite of the former Soviet Union. Churches were closed, and not even Mother Teresa was allowed to visit there . . . not even when her mother, Drana, was dying. "There are still walls that even love cannot knock down," she said. She continued to try to see her mother, but when the United Nations intervened on her behalf—and failed—she knew there was no chance of seeing her mother again. And on July 12, 1972, she received a telegram from her sister, Aga: "Today, July 12, Mother died at 5."

Deeply saddened, Mother Teresa went to the chapel and spent hours in prayer. She knew that prayer would unite the family forever, as her mother had taught her, and no government on earth had greater power than that.

Mother Teresa's love extends to children all around the world.

Not long after her mother's death, Teresa's sister, Aga, also died in Tirana, Albania. She had been living with their mother and caring for her until she died. Now Teresa realized "the two nightingales of Skopje" would never sing together again, and once more she went to the chapel to pray—this time for her beloved sister, Aga.

Skopje! Memories of her childhood home filled her head, and Mother Teresa wanted more than anything to open a house for the poorest of the poor there. (Though Yugoslavia was a Communist country by then, it didn't outlaw religion, as Albania had done.) What better way to honor the memory of her parents and her sister? The idea renewed her energy, and the plan to open a house in Yugoslavia became a high priority for Mother Teresa in the 1970s.

Mother Teresa's brother, Lazar, who had moved to Italy with his wife and daughter, kept in close touch with her, encouraged her plans, and praised her extraordinary ability to get things done:

> You could really say that she is the commander of a unit—indeed of a whole army. She has incredible strength of will, as our mother had. She is a conscientious and disciplined Catholic. This discipline is something her entire congregation has. . . . And she is their leader.

But it is the discipline combined with compassion that has been the key to her lasting leadership and remarkable success. "You just always knew she loved you," a co-worker said.

Mother Teresa arrives with Indian orphans in Italy to meet their new parents.

A Prayer for Peace

As Mother Teresa's missions grew around the world, so did her fame. Yet she always remembered her mother's words: "When you do good, do it without display." She disliked speaking in public and avoided publicity that focused on her instead of her work. She would always claim that thousands of others were working as hard as she was . . . if not harder. "Maybe so," one volunteer said, "but she is our inspiration—second only to God. . . . She's the one who made it happen." And because she did, the world has given her its highest honors.

Throughout the 1970s and 1980s Mother Teresa traveled around the globe to accept honorary degrees and prizes—not for herself but "on behalf of the poor." The more attention drawn to the terrible poverty in our cities, the better, she thought. The prizes include the Pope John XXIII Peace Prize (1971); the John F. Kennedy International Award (1971); the Templeton Award for Progress in Religion (1973); the Albert Schweitzer International Prize (1975); and the highest honor of all, the Nobel Peace Prize (1979).

After each presentation, Mother Teresa's comment was the same: "I am unworthy." And rarely, after accept-

Mother Teresa receives the Pope John XXIII Peace Prize.

ing an award, did she leave the podium without saying her prayer for peace:

> Where there is hatred, bring love.
> Where there is sadness, bring joy.
> Where there is discontent, bring happiness.
> Where there is despair, bring hope.
> Where there is wrong, bring a spirit of forgiveness.

But even Mother Teresa has had critics. Some thought that by setting up orphanages to house sick and unwanted babies, she was treating only the surface of the problem of poverty and doing little to solve the population explosion. Though she has opened family planning centers in India and other countries, only the natural method of birth control is offered there; artificial methods violate the tenets of the Catholic Church. And Mother Teresa calls abortion a crime that hurts everyone involved. "But we are not trying to do social work," she reminds her critics, "and we don't get mixed up in politics. . . . We are simply bringing love and compassion to the poorest of the poor wherever we find them. That is our mission . . . our only mission."

Like Gandhi, Mother Teresa has never lost sight of her goals and has been fearless in pursuing them. But when she decided to go to Beirut at the height of the Arab-Israeli conflict, friends wondered if she had lost her senses. "You'll never come back," they told her. But as long as people were dying in the streets and children were left without parents, Mother Teresa had to be with them.

Local leaders in Beirut were baffled by her presence,

Mother Teresa accepts the Nobel Prize for Peace.

and because she was so frail—and stooped-over from picking up thousands of children (42,000 in Calcutta alone)—they wondered how she could be helpful. But they soon stopped wondering as they watched her go into action in the streets of west Beirut. With gunfire all around, she treated the injured and comforted the dying. And she said a special prayer for peace. When a cease-fire followed, no one ever questioned her presence there again!

Mother Teresa comforts a child in war-torn Beirut.

A Messenger of Love

In 1978 another prayer was answered for Mother Teresa. That year, the first house for the poor—"who are hungry for love and for care"—opened in her native country, Yugoslavia. During her visit there she returned to Skopje, her childhood home. Many friends hadn't seen her since that day at the train station when the whole town, it seemed, had come to say good-bye to the young Agnes Bojaxhiu.

Fifty years later, as she walked through the town, Mother Teresa was filled with memories—memories of the singing and laughter that rang through the house where she grew up. But the memory of the homeless strangers who sat next to her at the dinner table was the most indelible memory of all. "They are part of our family, too," her mother had always said. With those words etched in her mind and in her heart she formally opened the new house in Zagreb, Yugoslavia.

In the 1980s more houses opened in Europe, Africa, the United States, and South America. *Time* magazine called Mother Teresa "a messenger of love" and gave its readers a glimpse into the life of "a living saint":

Between her travels to the Order's farflung outposts, Mother Teresa rises at 4:30 A.M., prays, sings the Mass with her sister nuns, joins them for a spare meal of an egg, bread, banana and tea, and then goes out into the city to work. Age and authority have not changed her; she is at ease these days with Pope and Prime Minister, but she still cleans convent toilets. . . . Mother Teresa's own loving luminosity prompts many to bestow on her a title that she would surely reject. She is, they say, a living saint.

Indira Gandhi, India's first female prime minister, said, "To meet Mother Teresa is to feel utterly humble, to sense the power of tenderness and the strength of love." And an American reporter wrote, "She is someone through whom the light of God shines."

In spite of a heart attack in 1983, Mother Teresa kept on working and traveling. On October 24, 1985, at the age of 75, she was the honored speaker at the 40th anniversary of the United Nations in New York, where Secretary General Javier Pérez de Cuéllar introduced her as "the most powerful woman in the world."

By 1992 she was overseeing more than 450 homes in

India's prime minister Indira Gandhi speaks with Mother Teresa.

95 countries on 5 continents! And although Mother Teresa has had to slow down after a second heart attack in 1989, she continues to care for the abandoned babies and the "poorest of the poor." Perhaps her whole philosophy can be summed up in a short conversation with a badly injured man found dying in the streets of Calcutta:

As she sponged off his forehead and bandaged his wounds he asked, "Why do you do this?"

And she said, "Because I love you."

For Further Reading

Clucas, Joan Graff. *Mother Teresa*. New York: Chelsea House, 1988.

Giff, Patricia Reilly. *Mother Teresa: A Sister to the Poor*. New York: Viking, 1986.

Greene, Carol. *Mother Teresa: Friend of the Friendless*. Minneapolis, Minn.: Children's Press, 1983.

Jacobs, William Jay. *Mother Teresa, Helping the Poor*. Brookfield, Conn.: Millbrook Press, 1991.

Mother Teresa. *My Life for the Poor*. New York: Harper & Row, 1985.

Porter, David. *Mother Teresa: The Early Years*. Grand Rapids, Mich.: William B. Eerdman's Publishing Company, 1986.

Index

Albania 13, 14, 34, 50, 51, 52

Beirut 56, 57
Bojaxhiu, Aga 13, 18, 22, 34, 50, 51
Bojaxhiu, Agnes Gonxha 13–20, 22, 23, 25, 34, 59
Bojaxhiu, Drana 13, 14, 16, 20, 34, 50
Bojaxhiu, Lazar 13, 14, 19, 20, 22, 34, 36, 52
Bojaxhiu, Nikola 13, 14, 15, 16

Calcutta 6, 8, 9, 11, 31, 33, 36–38, 40, 41, 46, 57, 61
Catholic church 13, 17, 37, 41, 56
Catholic Missions 19, 23, 27, 28
critics 56

Darjeeling 26–28

Entally 33, 38

Gandhi, Indira 60, 61
Gandhi, Mahatma 6, 9, 56

Hindus 9, 43

India 6, 9, 14, 22, 25, 26, 28, 38, 41, 46, 48, 49, 56

leprosy 6, 11, 47
Loreto Abbey 22, 24, 25
Loreto convent school 26, 27

Missionaries of Charity 6, 26, 39, 40, 41, 44, 47

Missionary Brothers of Charity 49
Mother Teresa 6–8, 10, 11, 13, 16, 17, 21, 24, 26, 29, 30, 33–41, 43–54, 56–61
Motijhil 38
Muslims 9, 41, 44

Nirmal Hriday (Place of the Pure Heart/House of the Dying) 44, 45
Nobel Peace Prize 8, 54, 57
nuns 6, 13, 28, 25, 36, 37, 46, 48, 49, 60

Pakistan 9, 41
Pope John XXIII Peace Prize 54
Pope Paul VI 4, 49
Pope Pius XII 37, 40

Shanti Nagar (Place of Peace/House for the Lepers) 47, 49
Shishu Bhavan (Home for Children) 46, 47, 48
Sister Teresa 28, 31, 33, 34
Skopje, Yugoslavia 13, 14, 17, 19, 20, 22, 23, 51, 59
St. Mary's School 31, 33, 34, 38, 40

Tagore, Rabindranath 45

United Nations 60

vows 27, 34

About the Author

Caroline Evensen Lazo was born in Minneapolis, Minnesota. She spent much of her childhood visiting museums and attending plays written by her mother, Isobel Evensen, whose work earned national acclaim and became a lasting source of inspiration for her daughter.

Ms. Lazo attended the University of Oslo, Norway, and received a B.A. in Art History from the University of Minnesota. She has written extensively about art and architecture, and is the author of many books for young people, including *The Terra Cotta Army of Emperor Qin*, *Missing Treasure*, and *Endangered Species*.